A People's Guide to
Houseplants

Cara Brezina

A People's Guide to
Houseplants

Thrifty, Sustainable Ways to Fill Your Home with Plants

Cara Brezina

Microcosm Publishing
Portland, OR / Cleveland, OH

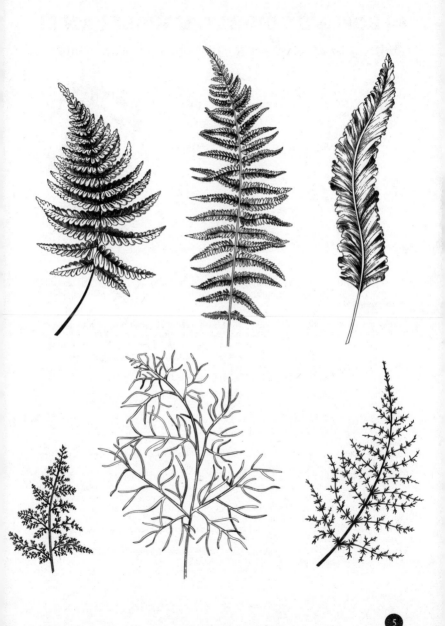

A PEOPLE'S GUIDE TO HOUSEPLANTS

Thrifty, Sustainable Ways to Fill Your Home with Plants
Part of the DIY Series

© Cara Brezina, 2024
This edition © Microcosm Publishing, 2024
First Edition, 3,000 copies, first published November, 2024
ISBN 9781648412875
This is Microcosm # 865
Designed by Joe Biel
Edited by Olivia Rollins

For a catalog, write or visit:

Microcosm Publishing
2752 N Williams Ave.
Portland, OR 97227

All the news that's fit to print at www.Microcosm.Pub/Newsletter

Get more copies of this book at www.Microcosm.pub/HouseplantGuide

Read more about plants and gardening: www.Microcosm.pub/Garden

Did you know that you can buy our books directly from us at sliding scale rates? Support a small, independent publisher and pay less than Amazon's price at **www. Microcosm.Pub.**

To join the ranks of high-class stores that feature Microcosm titles, talk to your rep: In the U.S. **COMO** (Atlantic), **ABRAHAM** (Midwest), **BOB BARNETT** (Texas, Oklahoma, Arkansas, Louisiana), **IMPRINT** (Pacific), **TURNAROUND** (UK), **UTP/MANDA** (Canada), **NEWSOUTH** (Australia/New Zealand), **Observatoire** (Africa, Europe), **IPR** (Middle East), **Yvonne Chau** (Southeast Asia), **HarperCollins** (India), **Everest/B.K. Agency** (China), **Tim Burland** (Japan/Korea), and **FAIRE** in the gift trade.

Global labor conditions are bad, and our roots in industrial Cleveland in the 70s and 80s made us appreciate the need to treat workers right. Therefore, our books are MADE IN THE USA and printed on post-consumer paper.

Library of Congress Cataloging-in-Publication Data
Names: Brezina, Cara author
Title: A people's guide to houseplants : thrifty, sustainable ways to fill your home with plants / Cara Brezina.
Description: Portland : Microcosm Publishing, [2024] | Summary: Want to fill your home with lush greenery? You can do it without breaking the bank or your back. Cara Brezina shares her love of plants and offers advice on how to choose, nurture, and not kill the houseplants in your life-all without spending a bunch of money—Provided by publisher.
Identifiers: LCCN 2024023020 | ISBN 9781648412875 paperback
Subjects: LCSH: House plant—Handbooks, manuals, etc. | Indoor gardening—Handbooks, manuals, etc. | Handbooks and manuals
Classification: LCC SB419 .B714 2024 | DDC 635.9/65--dc23/eng/20240822
LC record available at https://lccn.loc.gov/2024023020

MICROCOSM PUBLISHING

MICROCOSM PUBLISHING is Portland's most diversified publishing house and distributor, with a focus on the colorful, authentic, and empowering. Our books and zines have put your power in your hands since 1996, equipping readers to make positive changes in their lives and in the world around them. Microcosm emphasizes skill-building, showing hidden histories, and fostering creativity through challenging conventional publishing wisdom with books and bookettes about DIY skills, food, bicycling, gender, self-care, and social justice. What was once a distro and record label started by Joe Biel in a drafty bedroom was determined to be *Publishers Weekly*'s fastest-growing publisher of 2022 and #3 in 2023, and is now among the oldest independent publishing houses in Portland, OR, and Cleveland, OH. Biel is also the winner of PubWest's Innovator Award in 2024. We are a politically moderate, centrist publisher in a world that has inched to the right for the past 80 years.

Contents

Introduction: Dreaming of Houseplants

Somewhere out there, there's a houseplant for you.

I don't know what you're looking for in a houseplant. Maybe you're a nurturer hoping to see the plant thrive under your care. Maybe you appreciate the aesthetic appearance of plants and want them to enhance your room. The plants you choose convey your sense of personal style and even your own personality. Perhaps you want something green and alive close to you in your home to serve as a small connection with nature.

Plants improve air quality in a room. They add color and character. Some people consider plants to bring good luck.

I've enjoyed tending plants since I was a child. I remember my mother teaching me the proper method of watering plants when I was a tiny tot. I like watching plants grow, mature, and change, because there's always something new to observe or learn. It may be as simple as a particularly glossy and symmetrical new leaf emerging and developing. Or it might be a more significant change, such as a houseplant flowering despite all the plant guides claiming that it's a rare occurrence. Sometimes the surprises aren't pleasant, such as when a plant begins to languish for no explicable reason. Then I turn to research and problem-solving to figure out what's wrong.

Over the years, I've learned from my success with houseplants as well as some failures. One of my first plants was a spider plant in a hanging basket in my childhood bedroom window. I still have descendants of that original plant. Another profuse plant was a small, sad aloe that I bought at a yard sale. It survived and multiplied, and I've divided that original pot many times to share. My schefflera regularly flowers in the winter, producing bizarre alien blooms. I had a pineapple plant and an avocado tree that both produced fruit.

But I had another avocado that failed to thrive. I should have repotted it earlier and pruned it to encourage more growth. I once acquired a sago palm and figured

that I should give it a good watering to help it adjust to its new home. Big mistake—one that the sago palm didn't survive. For many years, I had a beautiful bird's nest fern that thrived with little attention. But when I moved, my new apartment didn't have adequate humidity to sustain it.

If you've never tended a houseplant, you may find this game of trial and error intimidating. You might be daunted by the idea of becoming a plant owner. There are a lot of choices out there, and tons of conflicting advice. Maybe you've failed in the past at keeping a houseplant alive, and you fear that you don't have that essential green thumb.

You also might be resistant to the high price tags of many of the showy houseplants you see in nearby nurseries and plant shops. The prospect of buying even a few plants can quickly become unaffordable. Combine overpriced plants with pessimism about their survival, and you might quickly become discouraged.

But there's still hope for you to realize your dream of a home brightened by thriving plants. A so-called

green thumb consists of knowledge about plants based on experience, not an innate knack. Anyone can develop a green thumb if they observe and learn from their plants.

You can acquire plants without spending beyond your budget, too. There are many means of acquiring good-quality plants cheaply or even for free. If you're a bargain hunter by nature, you may relish the challenge.

This book will show you how to do that, as well as how to maintain your plants easily and affordably. Most of the plants in this book are low-maintenance and forgiving. Many are easy to propagate—you can get more plants from them through techniques such as dividing them or taking cuttings. Most are inexpensive and easy to find. They represent a variety of different sizes, shapes, foliage types, and light requirements. Hopefully, you'll find the plant of your dreams somewhere in these pages.

In chapter 1, we'll start with profiles of a few foolproof plants that don't require much previous knowledge or special care. Then, in chapter 2, we'll explore the basic elements required to keep plants alive and thriving. Chapters 3 and 4 will look at different ways

to propagate your plants and display them to use your space to your plants' best advantage, no matter your living situation. In chapters 5, 6, and 7, we'll delve into a variety of creative options for affordable houseplants, including cacti, herbs, and plants that can be grown from produce scraps. Finally, in chapter 8, we'll close with a few pointers on keeping your plants healthy for the long term, such as repotting them and controlling pests.

As you read, you'll find that plant care isn't as intimidating (or expensive) as it may seem. There are just a few key points to remember: Every plant has its specific requirements, but in general, houseplants appreciate moderation. Not too much water, not too little. Not direct sun, but not complete shade. If you observe any potential problems with a plant, identify what it needs. Maybe it needs to be repotted or repositioned. Check if it's waterlogged, parched, or infested with pests. If you keep these general guidelines in mind, you'll be well on your way to a rewarding and harmonious existence with your leafy companions.

KNOW YOUR TURF

You'll be in a good position to spot bargains on houseplants if you're in tune with your community. Compare prices at different nurseries, plant stores, and garden centers. Does your town or city have a park, conservatory, or college with a greenhouse that might hold plant sales? Check out yard sales and community swaps. You may be able to buy some houseplants, especially herbs, at your local farmer's market. Keep your eyes open for unexpected opportunities. I once lived near a plant shop with limited storage space that would sometimes discard beautiful plants behind their building. Some of them were short-lived varieties, but I picked up others that thrived for many years after I adopted them.

Take advantage of online resources, as well. There are always local news sites and bulletin boards with information about events and opportunities in your community—the specific platforms tend to change from one year to another. Check out posts and groups on social media; you might be able to connect with people interested in swapping plants.

Chapter 1: Jumping In

*D*o you want to adopt a few houseplants without stressing out over research or preparation? Here's the shortcut section for the novice plant owner who just wants to visit a garden center, buy a low-maintenance houseplant, and plunk it on a shelf or windowsill without worrying about its survival.

The plants profiled here are common, affordable, hardy, and varied. Most will live for many years when provided with basic care, but they're not finicky. They will thrive under the light, temperature, and humidity conditions found in a typical home. Check once a week to see if they need water—for most plants, the soil should dry out to a depth of about an inch between waterings.

When you visit your plant center, you might be tempted to buy the biggest, showiest plant that catches your eye. Restrain yourself, and instead check out smaller specimens that are under a foot tall. Smaller plants are cheaper, and they're also more likely to adapt easily to a new set of environmental conditions. Also, many of these plants grow quickly, and they'll fill their niche before long.

As you're starting out on your journey, be mindful of the dangers that plants may pose to pets and small children. Some houseplants can be irritating or even toxic to cats, dogs, or humans if chewed or eaten, so if you have pets or children, make sure to research the varieties you're planning to acquire. Additionally, plants with spines or thorns can inflict painful scratches and punctures, and kids can harm plants and themselves by overturning pots within their reach. Plan your plant displays accordingly.

Chinese Evergreen (Aglaonema)

The Chinese evergreen has long, glossy oval leaves on long stems. There are many different varieties with different leaf colors, such as mottled pink, red, silver, or variegated shades of green. The plants are made up of

multiple clumps. The Chinese evergreen ranges from 12 to 24 inches in height, depending on the variety, and it grows very slowly.

Water: Water regularly and allow to dry out slightly between waterings.

Light: Indirect sunlight; varieties with darker leaves can tolerate lower light levels.

Chinese Money Plant (Pilea peperomioides)

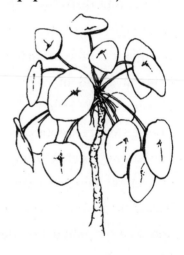

The Chinese money plant is also known as the coin plant, pancake plant, and UFO plant. All of these names refer to the plant's distinctive round leaves that resemble small water lily pads. The Chinese money plant grows to a manageable size of about a foot high and a foot in diameter. It's grown for its attractive foliage and, traditionally, for good luck.

Water: Water regularly and allow soil to dry slightly between waterings.

Light: Indirect sunlight.

Clivia miniata

Clivia has strappy leaves that emerge from a bulb beneath the soil. It grows from two to three feet tall. Its foliage is attractive, and the plant's flowers make clivia a standout. Clivia is sometimes called the fire lily for its spectacular  clusters of orange flowers, although some varieties are yellow. To encourage clivia to bloom, give it a rest period beginning in late fall. Place it in a cool location and water it minimally. Resume regular care once the flower stalk emerges.

Water: Keep moderately moist.
Light: Indirect sunlight.

Crown of Thorns (Euphorbia milii)

This shrub is a succulent—a type of plant with fleshy leaves that store water. These plants are adapted to dry environments and do not require much watering. The crown  of thorns has large spines protruding from its branches and stems, as well as thick, oblong leaves and clusters of flowers that are usually red but also come in shades of pink, yellow, and cream. The plant blooms throughout the year, although most types prefer as much sunlight as possible to produce an impressive display of flowers. Crown of thorns typically grows to about two feet tall, depending on the variety. Be careful when handling this plant—its sticky sap is poisonous and irritates the skin.

Water: Water thoroughly and allow to dry out partially between waterings.

Light: Direct sunlight.

Dumb Cane (Dieffenbachia)

Dumb cane is an attractive foliage plant with long tapered leaves in variegated green and cream. The common name refers to the toxic sap that can irritate the mouth and throat. Dumb cane can grow to over five feet in height, depending  on the variety. If it becomes leggy—tall and spindly with sparse leaves—prune at the top of the plant to encourage bushier growth. Alternately, you can cut it down to a stump about four inches high and it will quickly produce one or more new stems.

Water: Water regularly and allow to dry slightly between waterings.

Light: Indirect to filtered sunlight.

English Ivy (Hedera helix)

The same ivy that trails outside on walls and trees can also make an attractive houseplant. There are many different varieties, most with lobed leaves of different shapes, textures, and colors.

English ivy grows well in a hanging basket or trained to a trellis. It is also effective for purifying the air of mold spores and airborne toxins such as benzene. English ivy is easy to grow, but it thrives better in cooler spaces.

Water: Keep moist and do not allow to dry out.

Light: Indirect sunlight.

Fiddle-Leaf Fig (Ficus lyrata)

The fiddle-leaf fig is a showy foliage plant that has huge leaves—over a foot long—shaped like violins. It grows as a sizeable tree in the wild, and it will reach between 5 and 10 feet in height as a houseplant. Despite its name, the fiddle-leaf fig usually doesn't produce fruit when grown indoors.

Water: Water regularly and allow to dry out slightly between waterings.

Light: Indirect sunlight.

Hen and Chicks (Sempervivum)

The hen and chicks is another succulent. It has small, thick leaves with pointed tips that form the shape of a rosette. The parent "hen"  plant produces smaller "chicks" around its base. There are many varieties that come in different colors and sizes, the rosettes ranging from less than an inch in diameter to nearly a foot.

Water: Water occasionally and allow to dry out between waterings.

Light: Direct sunlight.

Peace Lily (Spathiphyllum wallisii)

The peace lily is an attractive plant with glossy dark-green oval leaves that grow on long stems and are pointed at the tips. Peace lilies produce white flowers consisting of a spike surrounded by a single  pointed petal. They are not true lilies—they're named for the flower's resemblance to the white flag representing peace. There are many varieties of peace lily, and they can range in height from one to four feet. Peace lilies are effective at purifying the air of pollutants.

Water: Keep consistently moist.

Light: Indirect sunlight.

Rubber Plant (Ficus elastica)

The rubber plant is a showy plant with large, thick, shiny leaves. Its name pertains to the gummy sap that oozes out if you cut a stem. The classic variety has dark-green leaves, but there are types that have reddish leaves or mottled leaves in various colors. The rubber plant is sometimes called the rubber tree—it grows as a large tree in the wild and can reach a height of over 10 feet indoors. Prune the ends of the branches in the spring if you wish to keep it a manageable size.

Water: Water regularly and allow to dry out slightly between waterings.

Light: Indirect sunlight.

Schefflera

The schefflera is sometimes called the umbrella plant for the shape of its leaves. About eight pointed oval leaves are attached to a single stem, which can be likened to the handle of an umbrella. The plant is a shrub small enough to set on a table when young and  eventually grows to about six feet or taller, depending on the variety. Some types have variegated yellow and green leaves. It's possible to grow dwarf schefflera as a bonsai—a miniature sculpted tree kept in a small pot.

Water: Water thoroughly and allow to dry out slightly between waterings.

Light: Indirect sunlight.

Swiss Cheese Plant (Monstera deliciosa)

The Swiss cheese plant is a showy and beloved household favorite. Young plants have heart-shaped leaves, but as the plant grows, the leaves develop holes and deep notches. In nature, the Swiss cheese plant climbs up trees or other vines. Mature plants are very large, with leaves  spanning 18 inches across and stems reaching 20 feet. You can either support the plant with a stake or keep it trimmed from the top to limit it to a manageable size.

Water: Keep regularly moist and allow to dry slightly between waterings.

Light: Indirect sunlight.

Zebra Haworthia (Haworthiopsis attenuata and Haworthia fasciata)

Zebra haworthia is a succulent plant with thick, pointed leaves that grow in a rosette around a central crown. The dark-green leaves are marked with bumpy horizontal white stripes. Most varieties grow to less than six inches in height, so the zebra haworthia is a good choice if you want a compact plant that won't outgrow its niche.

Water: Water regularly and allow to dry out between waterings.

Light: Bright indirect sunlight.

ZZ Plant (Zamioculcas zamiifolia)

The ZZ plant has striking and elegant foliage. It consists of multiple upright fleshy stems lined with waxy dark green leaves. The ZZ plant is a hardy and serviceable plant—it can tolerate low light and missed waterings, and it's known as a good plant for purifying the air of toxins. It can reach a height of about three feet.

Water: Water occasionally and allow to dry out between waterings.

Light: Indirect sunlight.

SAVING SAD PLANTS

Many garden centers have clearance racks with marked-down plants. Does this represent a great bargain for a savvy shopper or a potential waste of money and effort? It depends on the individual case.

Sometimes, plants are marked down because they're overstock or because they're flowering plants that are less likely to sell after their blooms have faded. These specimens are good candidates for rescuing.

Examine the plant closely. Does it appear healthy enough to recover if given proper care? Remember, being moved to a new environment will put additional stress on the plant.

A few yellow leaves don't always mean that a plant is beyond hope. It could be a reversible consequence of temporary mistreatment, such as inadequate light or humidity. Check the variety—if the type of plant is generally easy to care for, it may recuperate when tended properly. A finicky plant is less likely to recover.

The stem should be solid, not floppy or soggy, and not too leggy. There should be some healthy growth in the leaves. If they're mostly wilted or burnt, the plant is probably a lost cause. Take a look at the roots. They should appear white and feel sturdy if you nudge one with a finger. If they're mushy and brownish, they're rotten. If the plant is root bound—the roots have filled out the bottom of the pot and started to twine around each other—it will not thrive. If the plant or its roots smell rotten, you should move on.

Finally, the plant may be diseased or infested. Check the leaves for mold, pests, or damage.

If you decide to bring home a sad plant, don't expect immediate positive results. Even healthy plants may need time to adjust to a new environment. You may want to quarantine your new plant for a few days until you're certain that it won't infect or infest your other plants. Evaluate whether it needs to be repotted, and place it in a location with appropriate light and humidity. With time, luck, and care, your new plant will begin to grow and thrive.

Chapter 2: Basic Care

*T*he most important element for thriving houseplants—conscientious attention—doesn't cost a penny. Different varieties of houseplants have specific requirements regarding light, water, temperature, and humidity. Take these factors into consideration when you're positioning and watering your plant. Keep an eye out for changes that might indicate that you need to adjust the plant's location or care routine.

LIGHT

Houseplants all need sunlight to survive, but each variety requires a specific amount of light in order to thrive. The intensity of light in your room can range from direct sunlight to indirect light to nearly full shade. The duration of light depends on the length of the day, unless you're supplementing with artificial light. Flowering plants tend to prefer a brightly lit area, while some dark-green foliage plants will grow well in low light.

In most homes, the light levels inside will vary based on the exposure of the windows in a room—which direction they face. Windows facing south will provide plants with the most direct sunlight. During the summer, a southern-exposure windowsill is too harsh for many plants, even those that prefer direct sunlight. Some plants prefer to be placed a few feet away from a south window, where they will receive slightly lower light levels. Plants hanging higher in the window will also receive slightly less direct light because of the angle of the sun.

Eastern and western exposures both provide medium light levels. East-facing windows receive morning sunlight and filtered sun during the rest of the day, while west-facing windows receive the hotter afternoon light. Many sun-loving plants thrive when grown close to a western window, and plants that prefer filtered light will tolerate being grown slightly farther away from the window.

Northern exposures do not receive any direct sunlight. Shade-loving plants will grow well in a north-facing window with low light levels.

Your plants will let you know if they're receiving the wrong type of light. If a plant is not getting enough light, the stems and foliage may grow leggy. New leaves may be smaller and paler, and the plant may shed older leaves. If a plant is exposed to too much light, the leaves may appear bleached out, develop sunburnt patches, and even die.

Before you buy a plant, check the light requirements for that variety. Make sure that you are able to situate the plant in a place that receives the appropriate amount of light. Some of your plants may grow best if you move them around to different locations in your home depending on the time of year. Even if your lighting options are limited, however, there are plants that can thrive at every light level. Just confirm that the plant is suited to your location before buying it.

If you're looking for a plant that will thrive in bright light, try out:

Croton Plant (Codiaeum variegatum)

The croton plant is a shrubby foliage plant with thick, glossy leaves. It may produce bunches of small yellow flowers. The dark-green leaves are variegated with vivid yellow, orange, and red veins. One variety is known as Joseph's coat for its range of colors. The plant does not develop vibrant colors unless it receives ample sunlight, however.

If you buy a small croton plant, it may quickly outgrow your windowsill—the croton plant can reach heights between three and six feet, depending on the variety. Placing it on a plant stand close to a southern-exposure window should provide adequate light to maintain its leaf color. If your croton plant becomes leggy or if you want to shape it, prune it back in the early spring.

The croton plant prefers warm temperatures over 60 degrees and high humidity. Place it on a pebble tray if the air is dry in your home (you can find more information about pebble trays in the humidity section later in this chapter).

Water: Water generously; reduce watering during the winter.

Light: Partial to direct sunlight.

If you're looking for a plant that will tolerate low-light conditions, try out:

Pothos Plant, or Devil's Ivy (Epipremnum aureum)

The pothos plant is a trailing vine with heart-shaped leaves often dappled with yellow or white. It can trail from a hanging pot, climb a trellis, or frame a window. The vines can be pruned back to fit your space.

The pothos plant has a reputation for being tolerant of a range of growing conditions, including light levels ranging from indirect sun to low light. It earned the nickname "devil's ivy" because the plant is nearly impossible to kill. If you're choosing the plant specifically for a space that receives little light, select a variety such as jade pothos that can adapt to low light.

Water: Allow soil to dry out between waterings.

Light: Indirect sunlight to low light.

WATER

Appropriate watering is essential for a plant to survive and thrive. Both overwatering and underwatering can cause your plants to languish. There should be a gap of a half inch to an inch between the top of the soil and the lip of your plant pot to allow enough room for watering.

In general, most plants prefer to be watered thoroughly and regularly. They should not be kept constantly saturated, however. The soil should be allowed to dry out to a depth of about an inch between waterings. Water requirements vary widely from one variety of plant to another—check instructions for the plant's care when you acquire the plant to make sure you water it correctly.

Watering needs also vary depending on the time of year as well as the growing environment in your home. In regions that experience shorter days in the winter, plants' growth slows down. They receive less light and the temperature is lower, and they require less water than during the active growing season. But if you keep your home very warm, or if your plants are located near a heat source, you may not need to cut back watering as drastically. A plant's light exposure will also affect how much water it needs. A plant in a southern window will dry out more quickly than a plant kept in low light conditions. If there's a long sunny spell or an extended cloudy stretch, a plant will need more or less water than normal. Instead of watering on a set schedule, check the moisture level in the soil to see if you need to water.

For most houseplants, you can water from the top using a small watering can with a long spout. Water at the base of the plant and allow enough water to cover the soil within the rim of the pot. Some water will drain out of the drainage holes and pool in the saucer. Plants should not sit in water for an extended amount of time—after a half hour, pour out any excess water in the saucer. Alternately, you can use a turkey baster to suction off water.

Some plants, such as African violets, are intolerant of having wet leaves or crowns. Bottom water these plants by placing the pot in a basin filled with a few inches of water. Remove and let drain when the surface of the soil is moist.

Tap water at room temperature is usually fine for watering plants. There are a few plants that are sensitive to hard water, however, and water softeners contain chemicals that harm plants.

If you have a plant that's looking unhealthy, check to see if it's excessively wet or dry. An overwatered plant may have limp and browning leaves, and the roots and crown may start to rot. Too much water can also contribute to bacterial infections or mold.

A parched plant may have wilted and dried-out leaves. It may take a few rounds of watering to rehydrate it, or a long period of bottom watering.

If you're looking for a plant that loves lots of water, try out:

Lucky Bamboo (Dracaena sanderiana)

Lucky bamboo, from West Africa, isn't actually true bamboo. It resembles bamboo, however, with banded stems that are often grown in the nursery to form curls or plaits. It has widely spaced arching leaves and grows about two to three feet tall. If the plant becomes top-heavy, trim branching shoots a couple inches from the main stalk to encourage new growth.

Lucky bamboo can be grown either in water or in soil. If you grow it in water, you may want to set the stems in a few inches of pebbles for support. Tap water can be harmful to lucky bamboo, so use distilled water, bottled water, or rainwater. Change the water once or twice a month and top up the container as necessary.

Water: If growing in soil, keep moist.

Light: Indirect sunlight.

If you want a plant that requires minimal watering, try out:

Sago Palm (Cycas revoluta)

Despite its name and appearance, the elegant sago palm is more closely related to pine trees than palms. Long fronds emerge from a mounded central trunk. The leaves appear fernlike, but the stems are barbed and the leaves are spiny. In the wild, sago palms can reach 10 feet in height and  diameter; indoor plants generally do not get larger than

3 feet in height and diameter. The sago palm is very slow growing and is sometimes maintained as a bonsai.

Water: Allow to dry out between waterings.

Light: Bright indirect sunlight.

HEAT

Most houseplants have no problem tolerating typical room temperatures, but some varieties have specific requirements. Is a particular space warmer or cooler than the rest of your home? Is there a draft or a heat source nearby that will cause temperature fluctuations? Before you put a plant in one of these locations, check its care requirements to make sure that it can tolerate a particular set of conditions.

If you're looking for a plant that will appreciate a warm room, try out:

Ponytail Palm (Beaucarnea recurvata)

It's not actually a true palm, but the frondy leaves of the ponytail palm do indeed resemble a bound ponytail emerging from a short central trunk. Its long grass-like leaves curve upward and cascade  down past the edge of the pot. This plant is also called "elephant foot tree" because of the bulbous shape of its base, which stores water. The ponytail palm can eventually reach a height of over six feet, but it is very slow growing and will likely stay less than three feet tall in a pot. It rarely flowers, but when it does, it puts on a dazzling display of thousands of small flowers clustered in a plume.

The ponytail palm is native to Mexico and thrives in high temperatures. It is also more tolerant of underwatering than overwatering, which can cause the stem to rot.

Water: Water thoroughly and allow to dry out between waterings.

Light: Partial sunlight.

If you're looking for a plant that can tolerate low temperatures, try out:

Aspidistra elatior

The aspidistra is a foliage plant with large, oblong pointed leaves that extend directly from the rootstock. The leaves are generally glossy dark green, but some newer types have stripes or speckles. The aspidistra can grow up to about three feet tall. It grows very slowly and should not be repotted frequently.

The aspidistra has been a popular houseplant since the 19th century. It is known as "cast iron plant" for its ability to survive hostile growing conditions. Other nicknames include barroom plant and barbershop plant. The aspidistra can tolerate low temperatures, poor soil, sporadic watering, and low light, though it will thrive better if given proper care.

Water: Avoid overwatering and allow to dry out between waterings.

Light: Partial shade to low light.

HUMIDITY

Humidity is the amount of water vapor in the air. The humidity level in a typical home is fine for some houseplants, but others will thrive better with higher humidity, and some plants can't survive without a humid growing environment.  If your plants turn brown and shriveled at the tips and edges of their leaves, it's a sign that they may require more humidity. Indoor air in winter tends to be particularly dry. If you can afford to invest in a humidifier (or if you already have one), it will benefit your plants as well as your own health and comfort.

But there are also free or low-cost steps you can take to rescue your humidity-loving plants. Situate plants that need high humidity in the more humid parts of your home, such as the bathroom or kitchen. Grouping plants together can help raise the humidity levels immediately surrounding them. Growing plants in a terrarium also provides a humid environment.

You can set plants on a pebble tray to increase the humidity available to them. To create a pebble tray, place a layer of clean pebbles or coarse gravel an inch deep on a dish or tray that's several inches wider than the plant pot. Add a half inch of water, and place your plant on top of the pebble tray. You can set the pot on the pebbles directly or put the plant's saucer on top of the pebbles. Don't allow the plant to sit in water. As the water in the pebble tray evaporates, add more as needed. You can group plants on a pebble tray, as well.

Most experts agree that misting your plants will not help counteract dry air. The effect is temporary, and the water beaded on the leaves can be unhealthy for the plant.

If you're looking for a plant that loves high humidity, try out:

Bird's Nest Fern (Asplenium nidus)

Unlike most frondy ferns, the bird's nest fern has shiny, broad, curling leaves. New leaves unfold outward from a nestlike center. A bird's nest fern grown indoors is typically about two feet in height and  diameter, though they can grow larger. It reproduces through spores, which may develop on the undersides of the leaves. Spores appear as brown streaks on either side of the rib of a leaf.

Like most ferns, the bird's nest fern thrives in a humid environment. It should also be kept regularly moist, but don't water the center of the plant or allow the plant to sit in water.

Water: Water regularly and don't allow to dry out.

Light: Indirect sunlight to partial shade.

If you want a plant that will tolerate dry air, try out:

Jade Plant (Crassula ovata)

The jade plant is a striking succulent with fleshy oval leaves that resemble pieces of jade. It has a thick, twisting stem and branches, and it is sometimes grown as a bonsai. It grows into a shrub three feet or taller in height. Jade plants are slow growing and can live for decades. Because the jade plant has a shallow root system, it may grow top-heavy and benefit from pruning. You can also prune it to enhance its sculptural appearance. There are variants of the classic jade plant that have leaves of different colors and shapes.

The jade plant prefers a growing environment with low humidity. It actually increases the humidity in its surroundings by releasing water vapor into the air.

Water: Allow to dry out between waterings.

Light: Plenty of filtered sunlight.

IMMIGRANTS FROM AFAR

Have you ever wondered about the history behind the demure plant sitting on your shelf? Most houseplants are tropical or subtropical, originating in regions such as Africa, South America, Mexico, Asia, or the Caribbean. Some were gathered during scientific expeditions in the 17th and 18th centuries, while others were acquired by diplomats posted abroad. Ordinary Europeans were agog at the marvels brought back from the tropics, and in the 19th century, houseplants became more widely available for sale. Indoor plants became hugely popular, and certain species emerged as fads, such as ferns, which inspired a mania that swept Victorian England. Commercial nurseries were established to provide the public with houseplants, and they sent plant collectors across the world to hunt for promising new species.

Today's houseplants are the result of nurture as well as nature. Some plants on your windowsill might be familiar to their original collectors, but many varieties are the result of selective breeding. Horticulturalists and botanists cross different varieties of a plant in order to produce hybrids with certain desirable traits. Sometimes, they observe an interesting mutation in a specific plant and propagate it to create a new variety. Novel technology has enabled cutting-edge tools for this: scientists can now edit specific genes within a plant's DNA.

Joel Roberts Poinsett, a diplomat and botanist, was responsible for introducing the poinsettia to the United States in 1829. Unlike the familiar small shrubs you see displayed at Christmas, wild poinsettias grow up to 13 feet tall. Selective breeding has made the plants smaller and changed other traits, such as vividness of color and disease resistance.

African violets have also been extensively modified over more than a century of domestication. Originally brought to England from Tanzania in the late 19th century, this plant was found to be easy to propagate and quick to mature. Amateurs and professionals alike experimented with creating new varieties. Today, there are almost 20,000 varieties of African violet, according to the African Violet Society of America.

Interested in growing either of these old favorites? Poinsettias (Euphorbia pulcherrima) are the bestselling houseplant in the country, but most people discard them once their colors begin to fade. They're easy to grow as a houseplant, though it's more difficult to bring back their vivid colors for the next holiday season. If you want to maintain your poinsettia, cut it back drastically to about six inches tall in the spring. Place it in indirect sunlight and water it regularly, allowing it to dry out slightly between waterings. Transplant and prune to encourage branching if necessary. In the fall, the poinsettia requires at least 14 hours of complete darkness each day for two months if you want your plant to regain its vivid foliage.

African violets (Saintpaulia ionantha) have long been a showy and easy-to-grow favorite among houseplants. They range in size from dwarf varieties to larger plants more than a foot across, and the flowers come in many shades and can last for months. African violets prefer bright indirect light. Water your violet regularly, but do not allow it to sit in water and don't get the plant's fuzzy leaves wet when watering.

Chapter 3: Propagating Houseplants

*P*ropagation means growing more plants from an existing plant. There are a number of different methods for propagating houseplants, and not all ways of propagation will work for all plants. For some varieties, you might have a choice of multiple means of propagation that are all likely to be successful. For others, you may have fewer options and propagation may be more difficult.

On the whole, though, propagation is a fun, easy, and budget-friendly way to multiply houseplants. Often, a plant will need to be pruned, repotted, or divided during the normal course of its life cycle. Instead of discarding trimmings and offsets, you can plant them into their own pots. You'll end up with more plants for beautifying your home, sharing with family and friends, and maybe swapping—without needing to purchase them. You may be able to acquire new varieties of houseplants if you connect with other plant lovers interested in propagating and trading their own plants.

OFFSETS

Some of the easiest houseplants to propagate are the types that produce offsets. Also called plantlets or "pups," offsets are small copies of the parent plant. Growing an offset as a separate plant is often as easy as detaching it and planting it in an individual pot.

Here are a couple classic houseplants that are very easy to propagate from offsets:

Aloe Vera
The aloe vera plant is a variety of succulent that has thick, fleshy leaves that taper to a point and have spines on the edges. These plants can grow up to two feet tall.

Originally from Africa, aloe vera is used worldwide for medicinal purposes.

To apply it to a burn, cut off a leaf at the base of the plant with a knife, slit it lengthwise, and remove the gel.

Aloe vera plants produce small offsets that emerge around the main plant. When they're a couple inches tall, you can dig them up and start a new aloe pot. If they don't separate easily, use a knife to cut them apart from the parent plant. Allow them to dry for a week before planting.

Water: Water generously, making sure that the plant drains well, and allow to dry out between waterings.

Light: Bright indirect sunlight.

Spider Plant (Chlorophytum comosum)

Spider plants have long, thin leaves that arch outward from the plant's center. There are over a hundred varieties of spider plant, most marked by a yellow or white stripe running down the center of the leaves. It reaches about a foot tall, with a wider spread. Spider plants are ideal for hanging pots.

The plant is named for its hanging offsets. Mature spider plants grow long runners that produce small white flowers near the tips. After flowering, the runners grow small plantlets that resemble spiders.

Spider plants are one of the most effective houseplants at purifying the air in your home. They absorb formaldehyde, carbon monoxide, and other toxins and pollutants.

You can propagate spider plants by removing plantlets, placing them in water, and planting them in soil once roots have begun to grow out. Alternately, you can plant the plantlet directly in a pot of soil. The roots will take longer to become established than with the water method. A third option is to place a plantlet in a pot of soil without detaching the runner from the parent plant. Cut the stem after the plantlet is firmly rooted.

Water: Water generously and allow to dry slightly between waterings.

Light: Indirect sunlight.

CUTTINGS

Another means of propagation is to root a cutting from a houseplant. To take a stem cutting, use a knife or clippers to trim a three-to-five-inch sprig, cutting at an angle. It should include at least several healthy leaves and one growth node—a point at which leaves grow out. Remove any low leaves and place the cutting in a growing medium to root. The growing medium can be regular potting soil or water, or another medium.

A synthetic chemical called rooting hormone can encourage root formation, which may improve your success with cuttings of plants that are difficult to

propagate. It's commonly available in powdered form and is also sold as a liquid or gel. Dip your cutting in rooting hormone before planting. But many varieties of houseplants can be propagated successfully without the hormone treatment.

The cutting should root in four to six weeks. Keep the soil very moist during the process. You can increase the humidity in the plant's growing environment by securing a transparent plastic bag or clear container over the top. If you're rooting the cutting in water, plant it in soil when roots are about an inch long.

Stem cuttings aren't possible with plants that grow from a single stem. For some such plants, however, leaf cuttings can yield an entire new houseplant.

Here are a few very different houseplants that can all be propagated from cuttings:

Christmas Cactus (Schlumbergera x buckleyi)

The Christmas cactus is a joyous holiday tradition in many households. The plant produces a profusion of long magenta or reddish flowers with flamelike petals in the late fall and early winter. The Christmas cactus is not a true desert cactus—it is native to the rainforest of Brazil. It requires more water and less sun than a true cactus. The Christmas cactus has thick, flattened leaves that grow in segments. Although they're typically about 12 to 18 inches tall, they grow and add bulk every year, and older plants can reach a couple feet tall and more than three feet wide. Prune the Christmas cactus after it blooms to encourage branching. Christmas cacti thrive in hanging pots.

A Christmas cactus can be propagated through cuttings that are two to five segments in length. Allow the branches to dry out before rooting them in soil or water. Plant several cuttings in a single pot if you want a display that will fill out more quickly.

Water: Water generously and allow to dry out slightly between waterings.

Light: Indirect sunlight.

Philodendron hederaceum

The philodendron is a long trailing vine with glossy heart-shaped leaves. It's a versatile and resilient houseplant that's popular in offices and businesses as well as homes. The low-maintenance philodendron can tolerate a wide range of 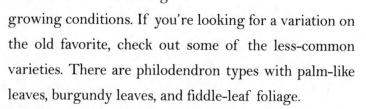 growing conditions. If you're looking for a variation on the old favorite, check out some of the less-common varieties. There are philodendron types with palm-like leaves, burgundy leaves, and fiddle-leaf foliage.

Philodendrons are very easy to propagate through cuttings from the vines. You can root them in either water or soil.

Water: Keep regularly moist.

Light: Indirect sunlight to light shade.

Snake Plant (Dracaena trifasciata)
The snake plant has tall spear-like leaves mottled in light and dark green, sometimes with yellow edges. It can reach a height of four feet. Some varieties of snake plant produce a lily-like flower, though they infrequently bloom as houseplants. The snake plant is effective at purifying the air by absorbing toxins and pollutants.

Snake plants can be propagated by leaf cuttings. Cut a leaf cleanly and allow it to dry for a day or two so that the cut end will form a callus. Root it in soil or water. It's even possible to grow a new plant from just a three-inch section of a leaf.

Water: Water occasionally and allow to dry out completely between waterings.

Light: Indirect sunlight to low light.

Tradescantia zebrina

Tradescantia zebrina is known commonly as zebra plant, silver inch plant, and wandering dude. It grows an exuberant mass of trailing stems with striped purple, white, and green leaves. The  stems of this hardy plant can grow up to two feet long. Prune any leggy growth to encourage the foliage to bush out.

The plant is easily propagated through cuttings, and you can root any stems that you cut off during pruning. The nickname "inch plant" refers to the distance between leaf nodes, which is a

helpful characteristic when propagating a cutting. Root the cuttings either in water or soil.

Water: Keep regularly moist and allow to dry out slightly between waterings.

Light: Partial sunlight.

DIVISION

If a plant forms clumps or produces masses of stems at its base, it's likely a good candidate for propagation by division. Remove the plant from the pot and separate it

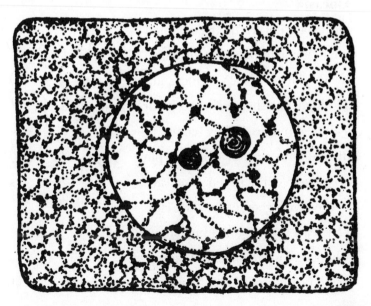

into two or more new plants. You can either pull them apart by hand, separating the roots, or cut the roots with a knife. Replant each new plant in its own pot—their new containers will probably be smaller than the original pot. Make sure that the base of each plant is at the same level above the soil as the parent plant. Keep them in lower light for a couple weeks until they've recovered and begun to put forth new growth.

Here are some plants that are easily propagated through division:

Alocasia

Alocasia is known by the common name "elephant ear" for the shape of its large leaves, which are wrinkled and heart-shaped with scalloped edges. They come in striking hues, from deep purple to glossy dark green, and are marked with geometric white ribs. The leaves grow on long stems produced by rhizomes—tuberous roots. Grown outdoors, some varieties of alocasia can

reach 10 feet tall, but plants kept in pots will stay much smaller. Alocasia appreciates humidity, so place it in a humid growing environment or provide a pebble tray.

Alocasia can be propagated by division. When you remove the plant from the pot, you'll find that it consists of multiple root clumps. Divide them by pruning them into sections and replant each in its own pot.

Water: Keep moist and allow to dry out slightly between waterings.

Light: Partial sunlight to filtered shade.

Areca Palm

The areca palm, also called the butterfly palm, has feathery arched leaves that curve outward like a butterfly's wings. It is sometimes grown as a plant with a single trunk that resembles a bamboo cane, though it forms clumps as it matures. The areca palm can grow to a height of three feet or more

as a houseplant, and taller planted outside. It is known as one of the top air-purifying houseplants, filtering out toxins such as formaldehyde.

Areca palms with multiple stems can be propagated through division. Remove them from the pot and separate one or more side clumps. They may come apart easily or you may need to cut them away with a knife. Replant the new plant in its own pot.

Water: Water generously and allow to dry out slightly between waterings. Areca palms can be sensitive to water containing fluoride.

Light: Direct to indirect sunlight.

Interested in propagating some of the plants mentioned earlier? Chinese money plant, hen and chicks, and zebra haworthia are easily propagated by offsets. English ivy, rubber plant, schefflera, Swiss cheese plant, croton plant, pothos plant, lucky bamboo, and jade plant are easily propagated by cuttings. Peace lily, ZZ plant, Chinese evergreen, and aspidistra are easily propagated by division.

SOWING SEEDS

Methods of propagation such as division and cuttings create new plants through asexual reproduction. The new plants are clones of the parent plant. In nature, most plants reproduce through seed, which is a form of sexual reproduction.

Starting your own seeds is an inexpensive and highly satisfying way of raising houseplants. A single packet, which typically contains over a dozen seeds, costs much less than a single potted plant. In the past, a drawback to this method has been a lack of availability of seeds for houseplants. Today, it's become easier to find a wider variety of houseplant seeds online, and to compare

prices. You can also check the selection at your local nursery and ask if they can order specific types for you.

To start houseplants from seed, fill a shallow container with growing medium—you can use regular potting soil or seed starter, which may improve germination and growth for some varieties. Make sure the container has drainage holes. Sprinkle seeds over the surface and cover them lightly with growing medium. Check the instructions for the specific seed depth and any special requirements for the plant, such as temperature and whether you should cover the soil with plastic. Seeds often prefer warmth in order to sprout. Once your seedlings have grown a couple sets of leaves, transplant them to individual pots or cells. Specialized tools or containers aren't necessary for starting seeds. You can even use paper egg cartons for planting your seeds or transplanting seedlings.

Here are a couple types of houseplants that you can easily start from seed. They're exceptional because, unlike most houseplants, they may flower and produce seeds that you can collect and plant to start a new generation.

Asparagus Fern (Asparagus Fern Asparagus setaceus, among other varieties)

The asparagus fern is not an actual fern—it's a member of the lily family—but it really is related to asparagus. The early shoots resemble very fine asparagus spears that produce frondy foliage with

needle-like leaves. With its trailing stems, the asparagus fern is appropriate for a hanging pot. There are several different varieties, one of which can grow vines up to 10 feet long. The asparagus fern produces small white flowers that may be followed up by red berries—actually seed pods containing several seeds—if pollinated. Dry the seeds before storing or planting them.

To start asparagus fern from seed, soak the seeds for 24 hours before planting. Germination will still take a long time, from two to four weeks. Asparagus ferns can also be propagated through division.

Water: Keep regularly moist.

Light: Indirect light.

Sensitive Plant (Mimosa pudica)

The sensitive plant is also called the touch-me-not. This unique houseplant has small, thin leaflets that normally lie flat on either side of a short stalk. When touched, the leaves are  triggered to quickly close inward, and the stalk moves downward. This is achieved by a change in the water pressure within the leaf cells. The leaf stalks of the sensitive plant extend from long, wiry stems with small thorns that can grow up to about 18 inches long. You can prune the stems when they become leggy to encourage bushiness. The plant produces a fluffy, spherical pink flower that matures into a small seed pod.

Sensitive plants only live for a year or two. To start a new batch from seed, soak the seeds overnight before planting. Sensitive plants can also be propagated through cuttings.

Water: Keep regularly moist.

Light: Direct sunlight.

Chapter 4: Displaying Your Plants

Once you own some plants, you can unleash your creativity in showcasing them. There are many different ways to display plants, depending on the variety, size, and light requirements. Materials can be bought new or used, repurposed, or constructed from scratch.

Displaying your plants can be as simple or as elaborate as you wish. You may be satisfied with a basic plastic grower pot, or you may want to craft your own vessels by hand. Perhaps you want to choose sustainable materials or repurpose interesting containers or furnishings. Spending more money on your plant displays doesn't make your plants happier or result in a more effective presentation. If anything, your own personal creativity is going to yield much more interesting trappings than buying drab manufactured products.

The most basic requirement of your houseplant is its pot. Plants aren't picky about materials—plastic, terra cotta, and ceramic are all satisfactory. The most important condition is that the pot has a drainage hole in the bottom. Place the plant on a saucer or drip tray to capture water that drains out of the pot. If you're grouping plants together, you can place them all in the same receptacle.

If you have a nice plant pot that lacks a drainage hole, you can use a drill to add one—a quarter inch in diameter is adequate. Alternately, you can use that pot or any decorative vessel as a cachepot, which is a slightly larger container used to hold a plant in a plain pot. If you keep a plant in a cachepot, make sure that it doesn't sit in water.

There are limitless possibilities for containers that might make interesting vessels for houseplants. You can make your own containers, such as decorative clay pots, by hand, or you can craft vessels to serve as cachepots. You can repurpose vases, wooden boxes, pieces of sculpture, vintage crocks, or even children's toys. Many different materials make good cachepots, including metal, ceramic, wicker, and fabric coverings installed on plain containers. If the material isn't watertight, nest a saucer or drip tray on the bottom.

The most common display method is a single plant featured in its own pot. But there are many different ways to situate a single plant. The obvious choice is a windowsill, but check the light requirements for the type of plant—the direct sunlight in front of a window is too harsh for many houseplants. You can place smaller plants on tables, counters, desks, shelves, and other pieces of furniture where you think a plant will improve your space. Many small to medium-size plants add lovely accents to your room—try a peace lily, jade plant, or crown of thorns.

You can also showcase plants on their own tables or stands. This is a good way to place your plant in a perfect position and at a perfect height to receive exactly

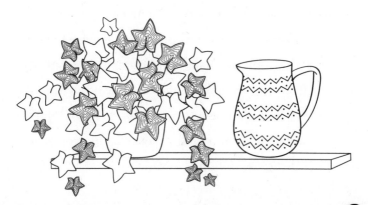

the right amount of light, as well as to add a focal point to a room. You can use a manufactured stand intended for houseplants or any sort of pedestal, stool, or table appropriate for your plant. Be creative—if you want something different, try a tree log, a step stool, or even an inverted wire basket with a wooden top fashioned from scrap wood. Many medium and large plants with a full shape look great on plant stands; these include croton plant, ZZ plant, and areca palm.

If you don't want your tall plant sitting directly on the floor, you can place it on a low platform such as a pavestone, a cork mat, a large trivet, or a plant riser. Plants such as Swiss cheese plant and fiddle-leaf fig are appropriate for floor placement.

Hanging plants provide another display option. If you want to add a plant to a room but don't have an open space on your furniture or floor, consider hanging it from above. You can hang a houseplant in front of a window from the window frame or suspend it from the ceiling. You can also position it close to a wall, either by suspending it from a wall bracket or placing it in a container designed to hug the wall.

There are many materials that you can use in hanging your houseplant. Hanging baskets are a popular option, as are fabricated hanging pots. You can also fashion a means of hanging a pot that doesn't have an attached hanger. It's easy to make a macrame or rope hanger by knotting strong cord or yarn—you can make your hanger as utilitarian or as showy as you wish. You can also buy or improvise a hanger out of sturdy wire. Regardless of how you hang it, make sure that your plant pot has some means of collecting excess water. If the pot doesn't have a built-in reservoir, consider placing it in a watertight outer container.

Vines and trailing plants are good candidates for hanging pots. Ivy, philodendron, ferns, and spider plants are favorites for hanging.

Another display approach is to group plants together. Choose plants that have similar light requirements. One basic method is to place several plants together on the same surface or in a tray. You might choose an arrangement of plants with contrasting colors, shapes, and foliage types, perhaps with one or two flowering plants in the group. Depending on the location, you might place a larger plant toward the back and a shorter plant in a smaller pot in the front. You can also group several large plants together on plant stands of slightly different heights. Or you might choose to group a collection of similar plants together, such as an array of succulents or violets with flowers of various colors.

A row of plants can also act as a living wall or room divider. Again, you have many options. You can choose an elegant lineup of the same plants or a variety of different types. You can place the pots in a trough planter, on top of a narrow bench, or in a row of plant stands of different heights.

Another way to add plants to a room without much extra interior space is to construct a plant shelf. You can put a plant shelf on a wall or beside a window, or situate it in the interior of a room. A plant shelf provides a great backdrop for showcasing plants of all different types, and it's easy and cost-effective to construct a plant shelf out of secondhand materials. Using Plexiglass for the shelves allows more light to pass through and can create a dramatic effect of uninterrupted foliage.

If you want a more restrained display of greenery on your wall, consider a trellis. You can install trellis segments on blank sections of your wall and train one or more vines to climb them. Good materials for a DIY trellis include wooden dowels or lattice, metal wire

 or mesh, or even rope supported by segments of metal or wood. Good vines for climbing an indoor trellis include philodendron, pothos plant, and English ivy.

CREATING A TERRARIUM

Terrariums have been a popular means of displaying plants since the Victorian era. A terrarium is a small houseplant garden planted in a glass container, sometimes enclosed. It can be as large as an aquarium or as small as a glass jar, such as a cookie jar. However, the sides should be high enough that they're taller than the tops of the plants. Although there's no minimum size for a terrarium, it's convenient for the top opening to be large enough to allow you to fit in your hand for planting and arranging the decorative elements. You can be as creative as your imagination allows in choosing a container, but it should be made of clear glass.

A terrarium can either be open or closed. The process is the same for planting either type. Here are the materials you need for assembling a terrarium:

glass vessel

gravel or small stones for the bottom drainage layer

activated charcoal

potting medium

plants

decorations

A terrarium is a great choice for someone who wants a unique and affordable means of displaying plants. You don't need to purchase a vessel or decorations designed specifically for terrariums. Instead, you can repurpose a food storage jar or an unused goldfish bowl stowed away in your basement. Check out thrift stores for a vessel or decorations, incorporate keepsakes as accents, or collect objects from nature. Clean the vessel and decorations with soapy water, rinse them thoroughly, and allow them to dry—diseases can spread easily in a terrarium.

You should fill about a quarter of the vessel's total capacity with planting material. Begin with a thin layer of gravel, for drainage, and then a sprinkling of activated charcoal, for filtration and purification. (If you don't have the materials, you can skip these layers without dooming your terrarium, especially if it's an open terrarium.) Add a layer of moist potting medium—regular packaged potting soil is fine—generally to a depth of a couple inches or deep enough to cover the root mass of your largest plant. If you want to shape the surface with landscaping elements such as rock cliffs or gullies lined by driftwood, place these before planting.

A terrarium typically includes plants with contrasting heights, textures, and colors. In choosing varieties, pick types that appreciate humidity and indirect light. Unless you're assembling a large terrarium, you should also select smaller plants that won't quickly outgrow the space. You can also include young specimens of slightly larger varieties that grow slowly.

Don't overcrowd your terrarium. If planting space is limited, you can use a long kitchen spoon or chopsticks for digging and placing plants. After your plants are installed, add accents such as gravel, shells, stones, twigs, or statuary.

Open and closed terrariums both provide humid environments for the plants, but a closed terrarium is more humid because it doesn't lose as much water from evaporation into the air outside the vessel. A closed terrarium may not need to be watered for several months or even longer after being assembled. If condensation no longer forms on the glass, it may need watering. An open terrarium will need occasional watering, but not as often as potted houseplants. A closed terrarium requires indirect sunlight—any direct sunlight can cause the sealed environment to become so hot that it damages the plants. An open terrarium also prefers indirect sunlight. Because it's not desirable for terrarium plants to grow quickly, you generally don't need to fertilize your terrarium.

Here are a few plants profiled earlier that are appropriate for terrariums:

Chinese evergreen—choose a young, small plant.

Zebra haworthia—a good option for an open rather than closed terrarium.

English ivy—miniature varieties are good candidates for a terrarium.

Here are a few more small plants that thrive in a terrarium environment:

Baby's tears (Soleirolia soleirolii)—a vibrant green ground cover made up of a dense mat of tiny round leaves on short stems.

Moss—various types of moss thrive in terrariums and provide a harmonious contrast to taller leafy plants.

Nerve plant (Fittonia)—a short creeping plant with leaves veined in dramatic white or red.

Polka dot plant (Hypoestes phyllostachya)—a compact foliage plant with oval leaves speckled in pink and green.

Venus flytrap (Dionaea muscipula)—a carnivorous plant with a gaping mouth, surrounded by trigger hairs, that closes on insects.

Many of these plants are easily propagated. Whether you're establishing your first terrarium or are an old pro, you can share them with fellow terrarium enthusiasts.

Chapter 5: Growing a Cactus Garden

Cacti make a delightful and distinctive addition to your living space. They are a type of succulent characterized by structures called areoles on their stalks. In almost all species, spines grow from the areoles. Cacti are native to the Americas.

Cacti only have one demand that may be difficult to meet—they require plenty of direct sunlight. Otherwise, they're tolerant of the temperature and humidity found in a typical home. Water cacti thoroughly and let them dry out completely between waterings.

Cacti are easy to start from seed, which is an inexpensive way to establish a unique assortment of plants. Cactus seed variety mixes are widely available. If you want to grow a particular type of cactus, check online for seeds for specific varieties. Cacti take at least a few years to mature, but the plants are interesting and attractive at every stage.

There are commercial potting mixes available for growing cacti, but it's cheap and easy to mix your own. In general, mix two parts potting soil with one part inorganic grit, such as coarse sand. You can also substitute other materials, such as pumice or perlite, for some or all of the sand. Cactus growers tend to have their own favorite recipes for growing different types of cacti. Check online for the pros and cons of different materials.

To start cacti from seed, fill a wide, shallow planting tray or pot with potting mix. Scatter seeds on top, spacing them evenly apart. Cover them with a very light dusting of potting mix—cactus seeds germinate better if exposed to some sunlight. Keep the soil evenly moist. Look for your first seedlings a couple weeks after planting the seeds, but be aware that some varieties may take up to a few months to germinate.

Check the specific planting instructions for your seed mix or cactus variety. Often, it's recommended that you cover the surface of the soil with plastic or seal the pot in a plastic bag to maintain moisture and humidity. However, though these conditions do help

seeds germinate, they can also promote growth of fungi and bacteria. You can sterilize your potting mix before planting by drenching it with boiling water or by microwaving the moist potting mix for a few minutes.

Your seedlings will pop up as two small, fleshy seed leaves. Place the pot of young cacti in indirect sunlight— seedlings may be sensitive to full sun. The first few spines will emerge within a few weeks to a couple months. Keep them moist for the first several months and then start to taper off watering.

After a year, cactus seedlings are large enough to transplant. You can either move them into small individual pots or keep them grouped in trays with wider spaces between plants. Be careful to avoid damaging the roots when you transplant your seedlings. They will be easier to extract if the soil is moist.

As your plants continue to grow, you'll need to transplant them again into larger pots. If you want to continue to group them in a single pot as a miniature garden, you need to take care in selecting the types of cacti you plant together. Pick small species with similar

growth rates so that your container will last for several years before the plants outgrow the space. Make sure that they all share the same watering requirements. You can decorate your cactus garden with decorative gravel, stones, figurines, or other accents.

Cacti should be transplanted every one to three years, with larger cacti requiring less-frequent repotting. In addition to allowing more space, repotting replenishes the soil. To transplant a mature cactus, the first step is to remove it from its pot. You can avoid being gored by wearing gloves or by swathing the cactus with paper, sturdy cloth, or bubble wrap. This will also protect the cactus from being damaged during the process. Place the cactus on its side to remove the pot. If necessary, loosen it by running a knife around the inside of the pot. If the plant is root bound, gently tease the roots apart.

Cacti have shallow root systems and thrive in pots that are small relative to their size. Transplant your cactus into a pot that's slightly deeper than the roots and allows less than an inch of space between the plant and the rim of the pot. Otherwise, the larger volume of potting soil will remain moist longer and potentially damage the roots.

After you've transferred the cactus to its new pot, fill the pot with potting soil to the original depth. Wait a week before watering in order to allow any damaged roots to scab over.

Do you want to see your cacti multiply? Many types can be propagated through stem cuttings. Use a sharp knife to cut off a branch of a cactus at a joint, or to cut a column cactus at an angle. Allow the cut to dry until a callus has formed. This will take a few days, or a few weeks for large cacti. Set the cutting in a pot of soil. Water it until the soil is moist, and then allow it to dry out between waterings. The cutting should begin to produce new roots within a few weeks.

Some cacti grow in clumps and can be propagated through offsets. Divide the clump when transplanting the cactus. Cut the offset away and treat it as a cutting— allow it to dry before planting it in a pot of soil.

Many varieties of cacti produce vivid, eye-catching flowers once the plants are mature. In order to encourage your cactus to bloom, allow it a dormant period during the winter. Water the plant less frequently and, if possible, move it to a cooler location that still receives full sun. Return the cactus to a warmer location and increase watering in the spring, when it is most likely to bloom. Look up the specific care recommendations for your cactus—some varieties are more likely to produce flowers than others.

There are nearly 2,000 different species in the cactus family. They come in a dazzling variety of shapes, sizes, and features. Here are several contrasting varieties that are popular and easy to grow:

Bishop's Hat or Bishop's Cap Cactus (Astrophytum myriostigma)

The bishop's hat cactus is a spineless cactus with pronounced wide ribs running down the length of the stem. The ribs are dotted with silvery scales. The bishop's hat begins flowering when it is just a few inches tall,

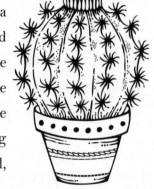

producing yellow flowers on top of its stem in the summer. A slow-growing cactus, it can eventually reach a height of about three feet and a diameter of eight inches.

Blue Torch Cactus (Pilosocereus pachycladus)

The blue torch cactus is a glossy blue-gray column cactus lined with areoles bearing golden spines. Growing wild in its native Brazil, the blue torch cactus can reach 10 to 30 feet tall and 2 to 4 feet in diameter, but it can take decades to reach this size. After it is at least 3 feet tall, it may produce showy white flowers that bloom at night.

Bunny Ears Cactus (Opuntia microdasys)

The bunny ears cactus is a relatively small cactus—no more than two feet high—that grows pad-like branches that can resemble a rabbit's ears as they emerge. They are studded with small freckles made up of tufted, hooked barbs that are very irritating to the skin. The bunny ears cactus is easily propagated through cuttings.

Golden Barrel Cactus (Echinocactus grusonii)

The golden barrel cactus grows as a sphere when small and matures into its namesake barrel shape. It has a thick covering of vivid yellow spines. Once the golden barrel cactus is about eight inches tall, it produces a crown of yellow flowers in the summer.

It can reach a height of two feet and a diameter of three feet in nature, but plants grown in the home will remain smaller.

Rat Tail Cactus (Aporocactus flagelliformis)

The rat tail cactus has long, trailing stems that can reach a length of three feet. It thrives when grown in a hanging pot. The rat tail cactus blooms in the late spring and early summer, producing big bright-pink flowers near the base of the plant and along the stems. It can easily be propagated from cuttings.

Rose Pincushion Cactus (Mammillaria zeilmanniana)

The rose pincushion cactus grows in clusters of globular stems covered with fuzzy white spikes. The variety is notable for its showy magenta flowers produced in a ring at the top of each stem. It's a small cactus, with stems growing about five inches in height and three inches in diameter. The clumps can easily be propagated by offsets.

THE MIGHTY SAGUARO

The saguaro cactus—scientific name Carnegiea gigantea—is perhaps the most iconic cactus in the United States. Its towering form, with upraised arms, is instantly recognizable. Native to the Sonoran Desert of northwestern Mexico and the American southwest, the saguaro is the biggest cactus found in the United States. According to the National Park Service, the tallest saguaro cactus reached a height of 78 feet. A mature saguaro can weigh more than two tons.

The saguaro produces white flowers that are pollinated by bats, followed by red fruit. In the wild, few seeds survive to grow into mature cacti. Saguaro seeds and plants are available for sale, however, and you can grow a saguaro cactus as a houseplant. They require the same care as other cactus species—plenty of sun and minimal watering. If you're concerned about raising a plant that can get as tall as a four-story building, don't worry. A saguaro seedling may only grow about an inch during its first 10 years, and a 70-year-old plant will be about six and a half feet tall. Saguaro cacti can live from 150 to 200 years.

Chapter 6: Indoor Herbs

Herbs can thrive indoors under appropriate growing conditions. They're an attractive and aromatic addition to a room and, of course, provide convenient, high-quality, and inexpensive ingredients for cooking. For many people, catching a whiff of fresh herbs when walking through a room can refresh their mood.

Every civilization in the world has used herbs for their flavor and medicinal properties. Growing a selection of various herbs represents a long connection to a wide range of different cultures.

If you picture an indoor herb garden, you're probably summoning up an image of a roomy planter full of lush, varied greenery sitting on a sunny windowsill. That's an appropriate setting for a healthy herb collection. Many herbs require ample sunlight. And when similar herbs are grouped together, they create a micro-climate that supports a pocket of humidity surrounding the plants.

Common herb plants and seeds are readily available. You can buy seedlings at a nursery or pay more for larger, established plants. Pots of herbs are sometimes sold in the produce section of grocery stores. Some herbs can be easily propagated, so you might be able to obtain cuttings or a root clump from a newly divided plant. It's easy to start herbs from seed, as well. You'll be able to choose from a greater range of varieties if you choose to plant seeds. There are dozens of different types of basil, for example, many of them startlingly different from Italian sweet basil. You might decide to try out Thai basil, lime basil, cinnamon basil, or purple basil. Pinch the tops off of young seedlings to encourage plants to branch out.

As with any other houseplant, you need to take light, temperature, and humidity into consideration when choosing and placing your herbs. Many herbs are originally from regions with warm, sunny climates. These plants may struggle to thrive during the winter at northern latitudes, where short days limit sunlight exposure. Situate your herbs in your sunniest window, preferably facing south, and rotate them regularly to expose all sides to the sun. Some herbs may still fail to grow well without supplemental light or humidity.

If you decide to plant several different types of herbs in a single container, choose herbs that require similar growing conditions. Parsley appreciates plenty of water, for example, but rosemary prefers well-drained soil. You should also consider the height and bushiness of plants when positioning them in the pot. Dill is very tall, for example, but it may be overshadowed by basil before it has a chance to achieve much height. Lifespans vary from one herb to another, too. Cilantro will go to seed within a couple months while thyme can live for years.

Herbs that only last a single season are called annuals. These are easily started from seed, although seedlings are readily available in nurseries, as well. Here are profiles of a few popular annual herbs:

Basil

The most common variety of basil is sweet Italian basil, which is used to flavor pesto and many other Italian dishes. Basil has glossy crinkled leaves that are oval with pointed tips, and the bushy plant can grow to anywhere from a foot to several feet in height,

depending on the variety. A mature plant produces spikes of small white flowers. Basil is a member of the mint family, and it was brought to Europe from India in the 16th century.

To harvest, you can pick individual leaves or snip clusters of leaves from stems near the ends of branches. Flavor declines after the plant flowers, so pinch off buds when they appear.

Water: Keep regularly moist.

Light: At least six hours of direct sunlight, as from a south-facing window, each day.

Cilantro

Cilantro is a delicate herb that grows fronds of long-stemmed leaves from a central crown. The plant grows a tall stem when it begins to form buds, and the subsequent leaf growth is smaller and lacy. Cilantro produces small white flowers that yield large round seeds. Cilantro is related to carrots and

parsley, and it is one of the earliest herbs known to be used by humans.

Harvest cilantro by snipping stems at the base of the plant. Don't cut more than a third of the leaves at a time. Cilantro will go to seed within a couple months, so you might want to start successive plantings in order to maintain a continuous harvest. High temperatures can cause plants to bolt, meaning that they go to seed early.

Cilantro seeds are the spice known as coriander. They can also be harvested after the plant has fully died back. Cut the plants and hang them in a warm, well-ventilated space to dry fully. The seeds may fall from the stems, so place the plant over a large plate or sheet of paper to catch them.

Water: Keep regularly moist.

Light: At least five hours of direct sunlight each day.

Dill

Dill plants are tall with a tough main stem and branches, and feathery, blue-green leaves. They produce umbrella-shaped clusters of flowers that mature into seed heads. When planted inside, dill requires a deep pot  to accommodate a long root. Indoor plants may need to be staked—they can be spindlier than outdoor plants because they receive less light and are not toughened up by exposure to the elements. Like cilantro, dill is related to carrots and parsley.

All parts of the dill plant can be used in cooking. The leaves lose flavor quickly after harvesting, and cooking at high temperatures also diminishes the flavor. Harvest dill seeds after the seed heads have died back and turned completely brown. Allow them to dry completely before storing them.

Water: Water regularly, but allow soil to nearly dry out between waterings.

Light: At least six hours of direct sunlight each day.

Parsley

Parsley is a biennial, meaning that it survives over the winter and then goes to seed the next year. It is usually grown as an annual because it produces a single tall stalk rather than leafy greens in its second year.

Parsley leaves grow at the ends of long stems, forming an attractive clump of foliage about a foot in height. There are two varieties: flat-leaf and curly. The more flavorful flat-leaf variety is prized in cooking, while curly parsley is preferred for garnish.

Parsley seeds are slow to germinate, and the seedlings grow slowly. When the plant is about six inches tall, you can begin harvesting the leaves. Select the outer stems, snipping them at the base of the plant, and allow the inner leaves to continue growing.

Water: Water regularly and do not allow the soil to dry out.

Light: At least six hours of direct sunlight each day.

Perennials are plants that persist for multiple growing seasons. When they're grown outside, the leaves die back in the fall and the roots send out new growth the next spring. You can dig up clumps of perennials planted outdoors and bring them indoors to grow them as houseplants. Make sure that they aren't carrying pests or disease before taking them inside. Conversely, you can set your houseplants outside during the summer and bring them inside again for the winter.

You can start perennial herbs from seed—although many are slow to reach maturity—or buy seedlings from a nursery. Many perennial herbs are easily propagated through taking cuttings or dividing the root clump, as well. Here are profiles of a few popular perennial herbs:

Chives

Chives are a member of the onion family. They grow in clumps made up of tiny individual bulbs that produce spiky cylindrical leaves that can reach a foot in height. The most common varieties are regular chives and garlic chives.

Chive plants are easily started from seed. To harvest them, snip the greens an inch above the level of the soil. Chives produce puffy lavender or white flowers that are also edible, but plants grown indoors may not bloom. In the winter, growth may slow and the plants may even die back slightly. Divide the clump and repot your chives every two or three years.

Water: Keep regularly moist.

Light: At least six hours of direct sunlight each day.

Lemongrass

Lemongrass is a showy tropical grass used in flavoring Thai food. It forms dense clumps that can grow to a height of five feet. When grown outside in warm climates, it dies back in the winter. Indoor plants can be maintained year-round, although you should prune them back at the end of winter.

If you have difficulty finding lemongrass seeds or seedlings, look for lemongrass stalks in the produce section of your local grocery store or an Asian market. You may be able to root these stalks, especially if there are a few roots already sprouting from the crown. Place the stalks in water. After roots have emerged, transplant the stalks into a small pot of soil.

Harvest lemongrass by snipping leaves or separating out individual plant stalks with a trowel. The tough outer leaves of lemongrass can be steeped to add flavor to tea or food. You can cut up the more tender stalks from near the base of the plants to use in cooking.

Water: Keep regularly moist and do not allow to dry out.

Light: At least six hours of direct sunlight, as from a south-facing window, each day.

Mint

Mint is a hardy plant that sends out a multitude of stems that produce dark-green crinkled leaves and small purple flowers.  There are many varieties of mint. The most common are peppermint and spearmint, and other varieties include chocolate mint, orange mint, cinnamon mint, pineapple mint, and ginger mint. The plant has been used for flavor and medicinal purposes for thousands of years. It belongs to the same family as basil, oregano, rosemary, sage, and thyme.

Mint is very easy to grow indoors. It has an extensive root system and grows prolifically to fill any available space. Plants grow to a height of two feet, but pinching the tops of stems can prevent the growth from becoming too rangy. Mint prefers moderate temperatures, so avoid placing the plant near a source of heat.

Harvest mint by snipping individual stems just above the soil. Flavor diminishes if the plant is allowed to flower.

Water: Keep regularly moist.

Light: Allow four to six hours of sunlight per day. Mint prefers indirect light during the summer and direct light during the rest of the year.

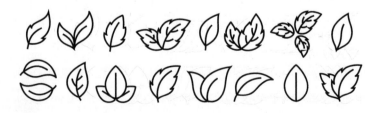

Oregano

Oregano plants produce a profusion of branched stems with fuzzy oval leaves and small purple or white flowers. Oregano can reach a height of one to two feet. The classic variety of oregano is well known in Italian cooking, but there are other varieties as well, such as pungent Greek oregano and a hot and spicy kind used in Mexican cooking.

Oregano grows well indoors. You can start harvesting sprigs after the plants are about six inches tall. The plants benefit from having the top growth trimmed back regularly to encourage bushing out and prevent them from becoming leggy.

Water: Keep moderately moist and allow soil to dry out slightly between waterings.

Light: At least six hours of direct sunlight each day.

Rosemary

Rosemary is an aromatic shrublike herb with woody stems, spiky leaves, and small flowers of varying colors depending on the variety. Rosemary can reach a height of over four feet, although it is slow growing and indoor plants may not grow as large if limited by the size of their pots.

Although rosemary can thrive indoors, it can be finicky about growing conditions. Rosemary requires a slightly humid environment, so you may need to take measures to provide extra humidity, such as positioning it on a pebble tray. The plants also require careful watering in order to keep the soil consistently moist but not waterlogged.

Rosemary is a strong-flavored herb widely used in Mediterranean cuisines. Harvest it by snipping sprigs off of the branches.

Water: Keep regularly moist.

Light: At least six hours of direct sunlight each day.

Sage

Sage is a small shrub with gangly woody stems that reaches a height of one to two feet. It commonly produces small purple flowers and oblong silvery-green leaves that are pebbly and soft in texture, although there are many varieties in a range of different colors. Prune back the plants in early spring.

Unlike with many herbs, larger sage leaves are as flavorful as younger growth, and the quality does not diminish after the plant flowers. Harvest stems or individual leaves. Sage is a favorite herb for seasoning stuffing.

Water: Keep moderately moist and allow soil to dry out slightly between waterings.

Light: At least six hours of direct sunlight each day.

Thyme

Thyme grows as a graceful clump of wiry stems that produce small leaves. Thyme flowers can range in color from white to lilac. The most common varieties are English or French thyme, which are favorites in cooking, but other varieties include citrus thymes and decorative thymes such as woolly thyme. Unlike many perennial herbs, thyme is compact, reaching only 6 to 12 inches in height. When the stems become  woody, prune the plant back to encourage new tender growth.

Harvest stems of thyme and strip off the leaves, or add entire stems to a dish and remove them before serving. Thyme adds great flavor to soups and complements many other foods. Some people like to brew thyme as a tea.

Water: Water generously and then allow soil to dry out almost completely between waterings.

Light: At least six hours of direct sunlight each day.

There's even a tree that can be grown indoors as an attractive ornamental houseplant as well as an herb source for the kitchen:

Bay Laurel

Bay laurel is a tree native to the Mediterranean region. It grows over 30 feet tall outdoors, but a bay laurel plant grown indoors is typically three to six feet in height when confined to a pot and pruned. Bay laurel produces tough, glossy oval leaves that are pointed at the ends. Outdoor trees bloom in the spring and the female trees produce dark purple berries in the fall, but indoor plants generally do not flower.

Bay laurel plants are available from nurseries. It's also possible to propagate bay from cuttings or start the plants from seed, but both methods require patience. Germination rates for the seeds are low, and bay laurel grows very slowly.

Bay leaves are used in cooking to season food, though they are usually removed before serving. The larger, more mature leaves have more flavor.

Water: Keep regularly moist and allow soil to dry out slightly between waterings.

Light: At least six hours of direct sunlight each day.

PRESERVING YOUR HERBS

If your plants provide you with a bounty of herbs, you can preserve them by freezing or drying. To capture the best flavor, pick herbs just before they're about to flower.

The easiest method of freezing herbs is to freeze entire leaves or sprigs. Spread them on a sheet, place them in the freezer for several hours, and then transfer them to a freezer bag or container. (You can skip a step and pack fresh herbs directly into the bag or container, but they will clump together as they freeze.) Frozen

herbs will retain their flavor, but their texture will be limp after you defrost them. They're best used within six months, although they will keep in the freezer up to a year.

Another method for freezing is to chop up herbs and pack them in ice cube trays. Place a tablespoon of herbs in each cube and add enough water or stock to cover them. Transfer the cubes to a freezer container or bag after they're frozen. These cubes can be added directly to dishes such as soups or stews, or you can defrost and drain them before use.

Similarly, chopped herbs can also be mixed with oil and then frozen. Blend them with just enough oil to hold the mixture together and then place the mixture in ice cube trays. Oil-based cubes don't freeze as hard as ice, and you can scrape off segments as needed.

Drying is another easy and effective means of preserving herbs. Most herbs intensify in flavor when dried. You only need to use about a third of the amount of dry herbs as you would fresh herbs. The exceptions are parsley, dill, and cilantro, which lose flavor when dried.

The most basic means of drying herbs is air-drying them. Tie stalks of herbs into small bunches and hang them upside-down in a warm, dry, well-ventilated space out of the sunlight. Herbs usually take one to two weeks to cure. However, herbs with higher moisture content in the leaves, such as basil or mint, may take longer to dry or may mold before drying, depending on drying conditions. If this happens, try an alternate method.

You can also dry smaller amounts of herbs in the microwave. Place your herbs in a layer between paper towels and microwave them for several minutes, stirring every 30 seconds or so. The specific time will vary depending on the wattage of your microwave. If the paper towels become soaked with moisture before the herbs are dry, change them.

Herbs can be dried in your oven, as well. Set the temperature to the lowest setting and leave the door cracked open. Place the herbs on a tray in a layer and leave them in the oven for three to four hours, stirring occasionally. Oven drying is a harsher method and tends to diminish the flavor and color of herbs. For some ovens, the oven light or pilot light is adequate to dry herbs overnight.

If you have a food dehydrator, it will yield excellent results when drying herbs. Follow the manufacturer's instructions.

Regardless of which method you use, test to see whether herbs are fully dried by crumbling a few leaves. If they feel crisp and break easily, they're adequately dried for storing. Store your herbs in sealed containers out of direct light. Herbs retain their flavor for several months at room temperature or up to a year in the refrigerator or freezer.

It's also possible to preserve herbs in oil or vinegar. For safe methods that won't allow bacterial growth, check out resources from an agricultural extension office—a resource provided by many a large university.

Preserving your herbs is a fun and satisfying activity! You'll also save money by not having to buy pricy dried herbs that probably aren't as high quality as your own.

Chapter 7: Plants from the Produce Aisle

*I*t's possible to grow certain fruits and vegetables from the produce you buy in the grocery store. Propagating these can be a fun project that yields interesting and striking plants. Even better, some of these are started from scraps that you otherwise would have tossed in the trash.

Avocado

You probably sprouted an avocado pit in water as a kid.

The novelty of the project often wears off and the plant never receives the care it needs to thrive.

But if you persevere, you can grow an

attractive avocado tree from the pit of the fruit. The favorite method is to insert three toothpicks into an avocado pit and suspend it in a glass of water. The pit should be positioned with the pointed side up, and the toothpicks angled downward slightly. The bottom third of the pit should dip into the water. Within a matter of weeks, the pit will split, a root will sprout at the bottom, and a shoot will emerge from the top. Transplant the sprouted pit to a pot, burying it so that the pit is half covered in the soil.

Alternately, you can skip the water step and simply plant the pit directly into potting soil. Leave the top third exposed. Keep the soil moist but not saturated. Avocados appreciate warm temperatures—they're native to Mexico, Central America, and South America.

Grown outdoors, an avocado tree can grow to over 30 feet in height. It produces long, glossy, oval leaves that are pointed at the ends. An avocado doesn't bloom until it is at least five years old, and it sometimes takes much longer. Flowers are small and greenish yellow.

An avocado grown indoors in a pot won't grow as large, and pruning will prompt the tree to grow bushy rather than tall. When the shoot is about a foot tall, trim back the top. As the plant grows, continue to prune in order to encourage new growth. Avocados grown as houseplants may or may not produce fruit, depending on specific growing conditions and care.

Water: Keep regularly moist.

Light: Place in direct sunlight.

Dates and Other Fruit from Seeds

You can plant the seeds of many of your favorite fruits to yield a plant. To sprout a date palm, for example, split date seeds and remove the nut from the center  of each. Wash the nuts and soak them in water for up to 48 hours. Place them between sheets of damp paper towel and transfer them to a plastic bag. Seal the bag and place it in a warm, dark location until the seeds begin to sprout, which can take from a couple weeks to a couple months. Dampen the paper towels again if they start to dry out. Prepare more seeds than you plan to plant, since date seeds have a low germination rate.

When the seeds have sprouted, plant them in a pot. Place them in direct sunlight and water them generously. Date trees are slow growing, but they mature into large palm trees when grown outdoors.

Here are some other fruits that you can grow at home:

Mango: Remove the seeds from the husk at the center of the fruit. Sprout your mango using the same process as for date palms. It will grow into a tropical tree with long, glossy, dark-green leaves.

Coconut: Soak an entire coconut and plant it in a large pot. It will take three to six months to germinate and will then grow into a large palm tree.

Citrus: You can grow fruit from the seeds that you remove from lemons, limes, and oranges. Simply plant them in a pot of soil. A citrus tree grown indoors may yield fruit after about three years, but it can take seven years or even longer.

Passion Fruit: Passion fruit comes from a tropical vine that also produces beautiful flowers. You can plant the seeds and grow the vine as a houseplant.

Dragon Fruit: Dragon fruit is produced by a flowering tropical cactus plant. You can grow the cactus from the seeds within the fruit. Two plants are necessary in order to pollinate each other and bear fruit.

Ginger and Turmeric

The ginger root that you buy at the store is actually a kind of stem called a rhizome. You can plant a ginger rhizome in a pot to grow your

own ginger. The plant also produces beautiful, lush foliage.

Select a fat, firm piece of ginger root with several eyes, which are the growth buds. If possible, buy organic ginger that would not have been treated with growth retardant. Cut it into segments about two to three inches long, each with at least two eyes, and let them dry for a few days to form a callus. If you bought your ginger from a grocery store, soak it overnight before planting.

Plant the pieces in a pot, with the eyes pointing upward, and cover them with about an inch of soil. Space them about six inches apart. Ginger is a tropical plant, and it will grow best if the temperature is at least 70 degrees. Don't overwater when the plant is sprouting to avoid causing the rhizomes to rot. And have patience. Sprouts will emerge in three to eight weeks.

Ginger grows into a clumping, stalky plant three feet in height with long, narrow leaves. It appreciates rich soil—if the leaves begin to turn yellow, it might be a sign that you should administer fertilizer or compost. After four months, you can begin to break off pieces of ginger from the rhizomes. The leaves will begin to die back after 8 to 10 months.

Harvest your ginger by digging up the rhizomes and cutting back the stalks. If you want to continue your ginger crop, select some small rhizomes and replant them. Ginger can be stored in the refrigerator for a couple months and frozen for up to six months.

Turmeric is a member of the same family as ginger, and you can grow and harvest turmeric using the same process as ginger. It's not as readily available as ginger, but some grocery stores sell turmeric root (which is

actually a rhizome) in the produce section. The plant grows slightly taller than ginger, reaching a height of about four feet. You can slice or grate the root for a variety of uses—drink it as tea, flavor your food with it, pickle it, or add it to marinades or dips. You can even make your own turmeric powder by boiling roots until they're soft, drying them, and grinding them finely.

Water: Keep regularly moist; reduce water when leaves begin to die back.

Light: Bright indirect light or two to five hours of direct sunlight each day.

Pineapple

If you've ever bought a whole pineapple from the store, you probably discarded the top without a second thought. If you'd saved it, you could have rooted it to grow a new pineapple plant that would eventually produce another pineapple.

To grow a pineapple plant from a top—the crown of the pineapple—select a fruit with healthy leaf growth. Cut off the top about an inch below the leaves and strip away the pineapple flesh and some of the bottom leaves, leaving a couple inches of the stem exposed. Allow it to dry for a week to prevent rotting.

Plant the crown in a pot, burying the stem up to the lowest layer of leaves, and pack the surrounding soil firmly. Water it thoroughly for a few weeks, until the plant has rooted, and then cut back on watering.

A pineapple plant has spiky, fibrous leaves with serrations near the tips. It can reach a height and diameter of three to four feet. Repot it as necessary to accommodate the roots. Pineapples prefer a humid environment, and you can place yours on a pebble tray if the air is dry in your home.

Your pineapple may flower after about two years, sending up a single stalk. About five months later, the plant will produce a single pineapple that you can harvest when it has turned golden brown. The original plant will die back, and you can now start the process anew with the crown of your pineapple fruit.

Water: Keep moderately moist and allow soil to dry out slightly between waterings.

Light: Keep in bright indirect sunlight while rooting, then transition to direct sunlight.

Sweet Potato

A sweet potato from the store can be sprouted to produce a showy vine that grows  well indoors. If possible, select an organic sweet potato that would not have been treated with growth retardant.

Sprout the sweet potato in a jar of water by inserting toothpicks into the tuber and half submerging it, with the pointed end downward. Within a couple weeks, roots will sprout from the bottom and plant shoots, called slips, will emerge from the top.

To transfer your sweet potato to potting soil, separate the slips from the tuber. Place the ends of the slips in a dish of water to root. When the roots are an inch long, plant the slips in a pot of soil. The vines will begin to lengthen and branch out, and you may want to support them with stakes or a trellis.

You can grow your sweet potato as an ornamental plant or, if you plant them early enough in the season for your particular region, harvest the tubers after three to five months. The plants will require a larger pot of loosely packed soil in order to yield a harvest. Allow the tubers to cure for a couple weeks in a warm place to improve the flavor.

Water: Keep regularly moist.

Light: Direct sunlight.

MICROGREENS

Most of the plants profiled in this chapter are slow to mature and require a lot of space to grow. If you're looking for a compact indoor plant project that provides quick gratification, you might try growing your own microgreens.

Microgreens are vegetable seedlings harvested to eat soon after sprouting. They're intensely flavorful and highly nutritious. They're pricy if purchased in the store, but you can grow your own on a windowsill.

You can buy packs of mixed microgreen seeds or blend together your own favorites. Microgreen packs typically feature a variety of different vegetables, such as arugula, cabbage, carrot, cress, kale, mustard, radish, and spinach. If you buy a seed mix, read the directions on the package—it may recommend that you soak the seeds ahead of time.

Select shallow containers with drainage holes and fill them with moist, loose soil. All-purpose potting mix is fine, and you can use take-out containers or disposable baking pans for your containers. Scatter seeds liberally on top of the soil, spacing them about an eighth to a quarter of an inch apart. Cover them with about an eighth of an inch of soil. Water them with a spray bottle and place them on a sunny

windowsill. Mist the top of the soil daily.

Seedlings should emerge in three to seven days. It's desirable for microgreens to grow leggy. The first small leaves are called seed leaves, and the true leaves will begin to grow about two weeks after planting. Your microgreens are ready to harvest when they have at least one set of true leaves—they will be a couple inches tall. Snip a quarter inch above the surface of the soil and rinse the greens before eating them. Microgreens are great in salads and on sandwiches, and they're also delicious in soups or on pizza. Cut microgreens keep for about a week in the refrigerator.

You can start a new batch of microgreens right away using the same soil and containers.

Chapter 8: Maintaining Your Houseplants

Many houseplants can live for years, but they'll be more likely to thrive if you monitor them conscientiously and tend to them as necessary. Maintaining your plants is not a particularly expensive undertaking. The most important things are to provide them with the proper water and light and to inspect them regularly for any problems. Prevention is the best way of keeping your houseplants healthy. Watch for trouble signs, such as yellowing, wilted, or dropping leaves. Common problems like these may be easily solved by changing your watering habits or moving the plant to different light conditions. Clear away dead plant matter so that it doesn't attract pests or provide a habitat for diseases.

REPOTTING YOUR PLANTS

In order for your houseplants to sustain healthy growth, they need to be periodically repotted. Young plants generally need to be repotted annually, older plants every two years or even less often, depending on the variety. Some types of plants, such as snake plant, grow better if they're not repotted frequently. Research the requirements for your specific houseplant before repotting.

Your plant will indicate when it's ready to be repotted. Roots protruding from the bottom of the pot are a telltale sign. Take a look at the roots inside the pot—if your plant has become root bound, it needs to be repotted. A top-heavy plant that topples over easily also needs to be repotted.

Often, you can tell when a plant is ready to be repotted because it needs to be watered more frequently. The roots displace soil as they grow, and water flows past through spaces created by the roots. If water immediately runs out of the drainage hole when you water the plant, the potting medium is not retaining moisture.

It's best to repot your houseplants in the early spring, before the start of their growing season. Choose

a pot that's no more than two inches larger in diameter than the old pot. Place a piece of screen or filter paper over the drainage hole to prevent the soil from escaping. Add a layer of moist potting medium to the bottom.

Water your plant thoroughly ahead of repotting. Remove it from the pot—you may need to loosen it with a butter knife or other thin implement. Dislodge as much soil as possible without disturbing the roots. Place the plant in the new pot, hold it in place while you add soil around the sides, and gently tamp down. Remember to leave at least half an inch of space between the top of the soil and the lip of the pot. Water the plant and return it to its usual location. Repotting can stress a plant, so you may see some wilting or yellowing leaves in the aftermath. Before long, the plant should begin to produce healthy new growth.

The planting medium referred to as "potting soil" often does not contain actual soil. When packed into containers, soil is too dense to allow drainage or air circulation. Most commercial mixes are blends of peat moss and other components such as perlite and vermiculite. Some potting soil blends are better quality

than others. Once you've tried a few different brands, you'll learn to recognize when potting soil is too dense or when it dries out too quickly.

You can save money and create a good-quality blend by mixing together your own ingredients. PennState Extension recommends combining one gallon soil, one gallon peat moss, and one gallon perlite, vermiculite, or coarse sand. The recipe calls for garden loam soil purchased from a garden center, but it's possible to sterilize soil from outside by baking it in the oven for 20 minutes at 200 degrees, stirring occasionally.

There are many different recipes for DIY potting mix, depending on what blend best suits your plants. Many houseplants thrive best in well-drained planting medium. Additional options for your blend include shredded bark, compost, and coir (a type of light coconut fiber). You might also consider mixing in limestone and fertilizer.

FEEDING YOUR PLANTS

Unlike outdoor plants, your houseplants grow in a potting medium without naturally occurring nutrients. Supplemental fertilizer can help your plant thrive by encouraging growth, supporting better health in the plant's stems and leaves, and increasing blooming. But fertilizer isn't an automatic trigger for greater growth. Too much fertilizer can damage roots and leaves. Most experts advise that it's healthier for your plants to under-fertilize rather than over-fertilize. They may even recommend that if you use fertilizer diluted in water, you should use a concentration slightly less than what's recommended on the package, or feed slightly less frequently.

You can promote healthy growth by fertilizing your houseplants during the spring and summer. There are many fertilizer options available. Either a general commercial formula or an organic option is adequate for most plants. Generally, plants should be fertilized once or twice a month, but some types of plants appreciate more feeding than others. There are specific formulas for African violets and cacti, as well as for flowering plants. Fertilizer is sold in various forms, too, such as liquid, spikes, and even sprays. Prices vary depending on brand, packaging size, and type of fertilizer, but water-soluble powdered fertilizer is often the most cost-effective form. You probably won't need to buy fertilizer very often, so watch out for promotions at garden centers or online when you're nearly ready to restock.

You don't need to fertilize a plant for several months after repotting. Some nutrients are present in fresh potting medium, but they will eventually be utilized or leach out during watering.

CLEANING YOUR PLANTS

You might not automatically put cleaning your plants on your list of chores, but plants can accumulate dust and other airborne grime. They benefit from being cleaned every few months. It helps with more than just their appearance—dust and dirt can hinder a plant's photosynthesis.

Cleaning your plant is as easy as spritzing or wiping down the leaves with water. You can spray down medium or larger plants by putting them in the shower or sink, or you can take them outside to spray with a hose. Use a very

gentle water pressure and keep the water tepid. You can mist smaller plants with a spray bottle or wipe them down with a damp cloth, or you can pick them up and dunk them in a bucket of water. Simply invert the pot, supporting the soil, and gently swish the leaves in the water.

Some plants, such as African violets, are susceptible to water damage. Brush them clean with a toothbrush or a small paintbrush. Paintbrushes are also good for cleaning between the spines of cacti.

PESTS ON YOUR PLANTS

You might be caught by surprise one day by the presence of pests damaging your plants. There are various ways that pests can travel inside. They might accompany a new plant from a nursery, cut flowers from a florist, or a plant brought in from the outdoors at the end of summer. Potting mixes can sometimes be contaminated. Sometimes there's no easy explanation.

Here are a few common pests that you might detect on your houseplants:

Aphids are small insects that occur in clusters around new growth and on the undersides of leaves.

Fungus gnats are small insects resembling fruit flies that you might see flying near the surface of the soil. Their larvae infest the soil and may damage plant roots.

Mealybugs are small, slow-moving insects that appear cottony. They suck the sap from the undersides of leaves and stems.

Scales are round or oval-shaped pests that attach themselves to leaves or stems. The insects are immobile, but their immature forms, which are too small to see, can move and spread.

Spider mites are tiny arachnids that spin dense webs around plant stems and suck the sap.

Whiteflies are small insects that resemble tiny white moths. They feed on the undersides of leaves and fly around when the plant is disturbed.

If you suspect that pests are damaging your plants, examine the leaves closely with a magnifier. Some insects, including mealybugs, scales, and aphids, leave a sticky residue on the leaves.

Catching an outbreak early on makes it easier to bring under control, especially if your plants were previously in good health. Immediately isolate any infested plants so that the pests will not spread. Remove any dead or damaged leaves from the plant.

There are numerous pesticides available to kill insects on your houseplants, but you may not need to resort to using harsh chemical controls. Start out using less-toxic options, which include many cost-effective treatments that you probably already have in your home. Remove all of the pests that you detect by wiping down your plants and spraying them with water. Scale can be removed with a toothbrush. Then mist the plants with insecticidal soap or a dish soap solution made of one teaspoon soap per cup of water. Other effective household treatments include mineral oil and rubbing alcohol, which you can apply with a cotton swab.

A single treatment will likely not eradicate all pests. There may still be a few that you missed, as well as eggs or immature insects. Continue to spray down the plants with water frequently, and repeat the treatment. Sticky traps can be used to deal with flying insects. To eliminate fungus gnats, allow the soil to dry out as much as possible without damaging the plant.

If the infestation persists, there are other relatively benign options you can try. Pyrethrins are low-toxicity plant-based insecticides. Various horticultural oils, mostly petroleum based, can be sprayed on to smother pests. Neem oil is a natural pesticide derived from the seeds of a tropical tree. Pest controls aren't cheap, but a small container of pyrethrins or neem oil should be adequate to keep your houseplants pest-free for several years.

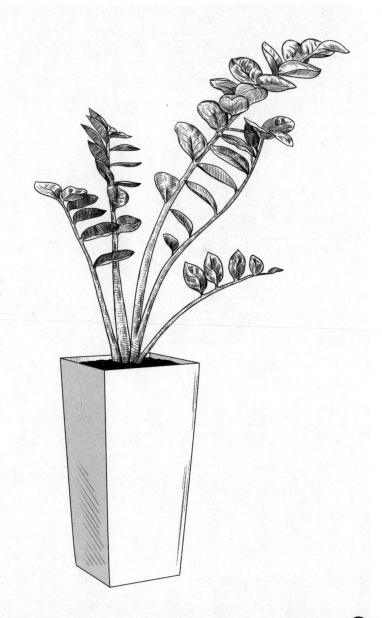

Most experts recommend against mixing together your own DIY fertilizer to feed your plants. It's difficult to achieve the balance of nutrients required for plants to thrive.

But there is another way that you can provide your plants with extra nutrients while reducing your own household waste. Setting up a worm bin is a fun activity that turns your discarded food matter into vermicompost—the result of worms breaking down organic material.

Starting a worm bin is inexpensive and easy. You can buy prefabricated worm bins, but a homemade bin is just as effective. You can find detailed instructions for constructing worm bins through internet resources such as agricultural extension sites, as well as in books about vermiculture.

One basic method requires two flat, opaque plastic storage containers. The size you need depends on the amount of food waste you produce weekly, but about a

10-gallon capacity is common. Drill holes in the tops, sides, and bottoms of both containers for drainage and ventilation. Fill one container about half full with newspaper shredded into strips one inch wide or smaller. Soak the newspaper in water and wring it out before adding it to the bin.

Not all types of worms are suitable for worm bins. The most common vermicomposting worm is the red wiggler (Eisenia fetida). You can buy them from worm

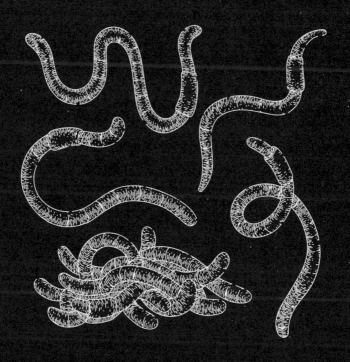

growers. The worms will probably be the most expensive item for your worm bin project. Check different sellers, because prices vary significantly. A pound of worms is adequate to process the food waste of a typical household.

After adding your worms to the bin, wait a couple days before you start feeding them. Worms consume most fruits and vegetables, as well as coffee grounds. Don't give them meat, dairy, oils, or acidic foods. Chop scraps into small pieces and bury them under a couple inches of the bedding. Don't add more food until the worms have processed their previous feeding. You can feed your worms once or twice a week, but the bin can survive for longer without feeding.

Place the bin in a location where it won't get too hot. Basements provide perfect conditions for a worm bin. Under the kitchen sink is generally fine, too. If the newspaper bedding begins to dry out, mist the surface to keep it moist. Add more newspaper as necessary. The bin shouldn't stink or attract bugs—if your bin becomes noxious, something has gone wrong with the environment.

Within a few months, your worms will have provided you with a bin full of vermicompost. If you're using the two-bin system, you can now fill the second bin with bedding and place it directly on top of the contents of the first. Begin feeding your worms in the second bin. The worms will move up through the holes in the bottom, leaving behind vermicompost that you can use for your plants. There are other methods of separating worms from the vermicompost if you don't want to use two bins.

Vermicompost provides a healthy range of nutrients for your plants. You can mix it with potting soil for planting and repotting—the OSU Extension recommends using one-quarter to one-third vermicompost by volume. You can also remove some

of the soil from the top of a plant pot and supplement with about half an inch of vermicompost buried under a sprinkling of potting medium. In addition, vermicompost can be steeped and strained to produce "worm tea" to feed your plants without disturbing the soil. Steep about a quarter cup of vermicompost in a gallon of water overnight—to boost beneficial bacteria, use non-chlorinated water, such as rainwater. Apply weekly or every couple weeks during the growing season.

Worms like **YES**

fruits and vegs leftovers

banana skin

apple core

potato & carrot peels

greens

used coffee grinds

used tea leaves

Worms don't like ⊘ **NO**

citrus   garlic   processed food   meat   fish

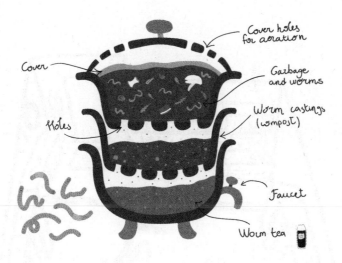

Cover holes for aeration

Cover

Garbage and worms

Holes

Worm castings (compost)

Faucet

Worm tea

Substrate

cardboard

paper

sawdust

coconut fiber

Conclusion

As you continue your ongoing houseplant journey, you'll learn from your plants and gain a new appreciation for their role in your home. Unlike some other forms of décor, your plants have personal quirks and their own stories of origins and survival. Maybe they help you feel more in touch with the natural world, too, even on a small scale. Your houseplants can even help you connect with other people, especially plant lovers who support making plants accessible to all through sharing and swapping. Whether you're content owning a single houseplant or feel the need to nurture as many as your home can hold, you'll find that houseplants are a source of joy that you share with others around you no matter where you are.

Recommended Resources

BOOKS

Want to know more? I suggest taking advantage of another affordable resource—your local public library. Here are a few books that I consulted when researching this book. I recommend them if you seek to examine houseplant topics in greater depth.

Anderson, Miles. *The Complete Guide to Growing Cacti and Succulents: A Comprehensive Guide to Identification, Care and Cultivation*. Lanham, MD: Lorenz Books, 2003.

Baker, Sandy. *The Complete Guide to Keeping Your Houseplants Alive and Thriving: Everything You Need to Know Explained Simply*. Ocala, FL: Atlantic Publishing Group, Inc., 2012.

Betz, Susan. *Herbal Houseplants: Grow Beautiful Herbs—Indoors!* Beverly, MA: Quarto Publishing Group, 2021.

Hessayon, D. G. *The Houseplant Expert.* New York: Sterling Publishing Co. Inc., 1996.

Horst, Danae. *Houseplants for All: How to Fill Any Home with Happy Plants.* Boston: Houghton Mifflin Harcourt, 2020.

Martin, Tovah. *The Indestructible Houseplant: 200 Beautiful Plants That Everyone Can Grow.* Portland, OR: Timber Press, 2015.

McHoy, Peter. *An Illustrated A–Z Guide to Houseplants: Everything You Need to Know to Identify, Choose and Care for 350 of the Most Popular Houseplants.* Lanham, MD: Lorenz Books, 2013.

Rees, Paul. *The Kew Gardener's Guide to Growing Cacti and Succulents: The Art and Science to Grow with Confidence.* London: Frances Lincoln, 2023.

Steinkopf, Lisa Eldred. *Houseplants: The Complete Guide to Choosing, Growing and Caring for Indoor Plants.* Minneapolis: Quarto Publishing Group, 2017.

Westhorpe, Tamsin. *Grow Houseplants: Essential Know-How and Expert Advice for Gardening Success.* DK Publishing: 2021.

Zachos, Ellen. *Growing Healthy Houseplants: Choose the Right Plant, Water Wisely, and Control Pests.* North Adams, MA: Storey Publishing, 2014.

ONLINE RESOURCES

If you get your specialist houseplant info online, look for reliable sources. The American Horticultural Society (ahsgardening.org) is a valuable resource for houseplant enthusiasts. The agricultural extension offices associated with many public universities provide a wealth of information about agriculture, gardening, food safety, and more, including many articles on houseplants. Botanical gardens also provide helpful information to the public. Here are a few articles that I consulted when researching topics in this book and can recommend if you want more information:

Chamberland, Michael. "The Terrarium—An Oasis of Humidity for Plants." The University of Arizona

Cooperative Extension. May 2023. extension.arizona.
edu/sites/extension.arizona.edu/files/pubs/az2050-
2023.pdf.

"Cheap and Easy Worm Bin." WSU Extension. Accessed
July 15, 2024. https://extension.wsu.edu/whatcom/
hg/cheap-and-easy-worm-bin/.

Hamilton, Douglas W. "Vermicomposting—Composting
with Worms." OSU Extension. March 2017.
extension.okstate.edu/fact-sheets/vermicomposting-
composting-with-worms.html.

"Herbs Are Easy to Grow Indoors in the Winter." OSU
Extension. November 19, 2023. extension.okstate.
edu/announcements/grow-gardening-columns/
november-19-2023.html.

"Home Propagation of Houseplants." MU Extension.
May 2022. extension.missouri.edu/publications/
g6560.

Horney, Julie. "Grow Microgreens at Home." Purdue
University Extension. February 1, 2022. extension.

purdue.edu/news/county/allen/2022/02/grow-microgreens-at-home.html.

Bunning, M. et al. "Herbs: Preserving and Using." Colorado State University Extension. October 2014. extension.colostate.edu/topic-areas/nutrition-food-safety-health/herbs-preserving-and-using-9-335/.

"Saguaro Cactus." Organ Pipe Cactus National Monument, Arizona. Accessed July 15, 2024. nps.gov/orpi/learn/nature/saguaro-cactus.htm.

Sellmer, Jim, and Kathy Kelley. "Homemade Potting Media." PennState Extension. March 14, 2023. extension.psu.edu/homemade-potting-media.

Karen Zaworski. "Fresh All Winter: Grow Herbs Indoors." Chicago Botanic Garden. Accessed July 15, 2024. chicagobotanic.org/plantinfo/smartgardener/fresh_all_winter_grow_herbs_indoors.

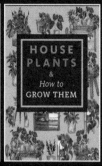